CELEBRATING THE FAMILY NAME OF DIXON

Celebrating the Family Name of Dixon

Walter the Educator

Silent King Books
a WhichHead Entertainment Imprint

Copyright © 2024 by Walter the Educator

All rights reserved. No part of this book may be reproduced in any manner whatsoever without written permission except in the case of brief quotations embodied in critical articles and reviews.

First Printing, 2024

Disclaimer

This book is a literary work; the story is not about specific persons, locations, situations, and/or circumstances unless mentioned in a historical context. Any resemblance to real persons, locations, situations, and/or circumstances is coincidental. This book is for entertainment and informational purposes only. The author and publisher offer this information without warranties expressed or implied. No matter the grounds, neither the author nor the publisher will be accountable for any losses, injuries, or other damages caused by the reader's use of this book. The use of this book acknowledges an understanding and acceptance of this disclaimer.

Celebrating the Family Name of Dixon is a memory book that belongs to the Celebrating Family Name Book Series by Walter the Educator. Collect them all and more books at WaltertheEducator.com

USE THE EXTRA SPACE TO DOCUMENT YOUR FAMILY MEMORIES THROUGHOUT THE YEARS

DIXON

From roots that run deep, in lands far and wide,

Celebrating the Family Name of

Dixon

The Dixon name stands, a banner of pride.

With courage and wisdom through years they have grown,

A family united, where love is home.

Through valleys and mountains, in sun and in rain,

The Dixons have journeyed with strength to sustain.

Generations of voices, now echoes in time,

Each telling a story, in rhythm and rhyme.

The Dixon name rises like stars in the night,

A beacon of honor, glowing with light.

With hearts that are steady, with spirits that soar,

They open each chapter, prepared to explore.

The first of their kin who carved out the way,

Built with their hands, with no thought to sway.

From humble beginnings to dreams that would grow,

The Dixons forged onward through rivers that flow.

Celebrating the Family Name of

In the heart of each Dixon is a fire untamed,

A passion for justice, for progress unclaimed.

With voices that speak for the voiceless, they stand,

A symbol of strength, a guiding hand.

In the quiet of dawn, or the dusk's fading hue,

The Dixons remember the ties that are true.

For family is more than just bloodlines entwined,

It's the love and the loyalty that forever bind.

And though time may change, and seasons may turn,

The Dixon flame continues to burn.

With laughter and joy, with tears that are shed,

They honor the living, and remember the dead.

Each Dixon that comes brings a new kind of grace,

Adding their name to the family's embrace.

From teachers to leaders, from dreamers to doers,

Their hearts are as vast as the wildest of shores.

In moments of triumph, in battles of strife,

The Dixons have weathered the tempests of life.

They've danced in the joy, they've sung in the pain,

Celebrating the Family Name of

Dixon

And through it all, they've risen again.

With hands that build bridges, with minds that inspire,

The Dixons ignite the world's quiet fire.

Not seeking for glory, nor riches, nor fame,

But leaving a legacy wrapped in their name.

ABOUT THE CREATOR

Walter the Educator is one of the pseudonyms for Walter Anderson. Formally educated in Chemistry, Business, and Education, he is an educator, an author, a diverse entrepreneur, and he is the son of a disabled war veteran. "Walter the Educator" shares his time between educating and creating. He holds interests and owns several creative projects that entertain, enlighten, enhance, and educate, hoping to inspire and motivate you. Follow, find new works, and stay up to date with Walter the Educator™

at WaltertheEducator.com

Milton Keynes UK
Ingram Content Group UK Ltd.
UKHW032323121024
449589UK00010B/374